MANAGING MEETINGS

TIM HINDLE

DORLING KINDERSLEY
London • New York • Sydney • Moscow

A DORLING KINDERSLEY BOOK

Project Editor Sasha Heseltine
Editor David Tombesi-Walton
Designers Elaine C. Monaghan,
Austin Barlow
Assistant Editor Felicity Crowe
Assistant Designer Laura Watson

DTP Designer Jason Little
Production Controller Silvia La Greca

Series Editor Jane Simmonds
Series Art Editor Jayne Jones

Managing Editor Stephanie Jackson
Managing Art Editor Nigel Duffield

First published in Great Britain in 1998
by Dorling Kindersley Limited,
9 Henrietta Street,
London WC2E 8PS

4 6 8 10 9 7 5

Copyright © 1998
Dorling Kindersley Limited, London
Text copyright © 1998 Tim Hindle

Visit us on the World Wide Web at
http://www.dk.com

A CIP catalogue record for this book is available
from the British Library

ISBN 0 7513 0529 4

Reproduced by Colourscan, Singapore
Printed in Hong Kong by Wing King Tong Co. Ltd.

CONTENTS

INTRODUCTION

Meetings are a crucial element of business, with millions being held all over the world every day. Managing Meetings will help you to improve your handling of meetings – whether you are attending as a participant or as the chairperson – so that they run efficiently and effectively. Practical advice is given on all aspects of holding formal and informal meetings, from essential preparation, to appropriate seating, to keeping on schedule, to final closing. 101 concise tips are scattered throughout the book to give further vital information on how to achieve your aims. A self-assessment exercise allows you to evaluate and chart your progress regularly. This book provides invaluable advice that you will be able to utilize time and time again as you increase your ability to manage meetings successfully and with confidence.

USING MEETINGS EFFECTIVELY

Meetings cost time and money, both of which are valuable. Hold meetings only when necessary, and ensure that they are concise and constructive.

DO YOU NEED A MEETING?

Most managers feel pressurized by the amount of time that they are expected to spend in meetings. But how many meetings really serve a useful purpose? If you were to consider the true cost of meetings, you might arrange – and attend – fewer of them.

DEFINING MEETINGS

A business meeting consists of people coming together for the purpose of resolving problems or making decisions. A casual encounter in the corridor between colleagues could be described as a meeting. However, most meetings at work are more formal, with a prearranged time and venue. They may be one-to-one meetings with a senior manager, colleague, or client, but usually they consist of more than two people. The typical meeting has a clearly defined purpose summarized in an agenda – a written list of issues to be discussed – that is circulated in advance.

Sales manager helps put information in context

Sales representative presents report

CONSIDERING COSTS

The best meetings save time and money by bringing together the right people to pool their knowledge for a defined purpose. However, many meetings are held unnecessarily – for example, the regular team meeting that once had a purpose then became a habit, or the meeting seen as a break from working alone. These are expensive luxuries. The biggest cost of any meeting is usually that of the participants' time – from reading the agenda and preparing materials, to attending the meeting. If participants will have to travel, this time must also be taken into account. Finally, there is the "opportunity cost": what could the participants have been doing if they had not been in the meeting, and how much would that have been worth to their organization? Consider all these costs before calling a meeting.

ADDING UP COSTS

To work out a meeting's total cost, first calculate the combined salaries of all the participants. Add to this the annual cost of their respective organizations' overheads, and divide the sum by the number of working hours there are in a year (working hours per week multiplied by working weeks per year). Add any sundry hourly costs, such as room hire. This final total is the cost per hour of the meeting. Is the purpose of the meeting really worth that much money? It may well be; but you should always consider less costly but equally effective alternatives.

Managing director chairs meeting

Sales director puts questions to sales team

Secretary takes minutes

◀ **HOLDING A MEETING**

This meeting brings together members of a department and a managing director in order to resolve an issue. Based on their combined salaries of £180,000 a year, annual overheads of £100,000, and various sundry costs, the hourly cost of this meeting is £178.

KNOWING YOUR AIMS

Meetings can be held for any number of different reasons. The exact purpose of a meeting must always be made clear well in advance to both the chairperson and the participants. This helps everyone to make the meeting a success.

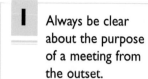

1 Always be clear about the purpose of a meeting from the outset.

CONSIDERING PURPOSE

The purpose of most meetings will fall into one of the following categories. Decide in advance to which of these a particular meeting will belong, and ensure that all participants are aware of it:

2 If an issue can be resolved without a meeting, cancel the meeting.

- Imparting information or advice;
- Issuing instructions;
- Addressing grievances or arbitrating;
- Making or implementing decisions;
- Generating creative ideas;
- Presenting a proposal for discussion and, usually, for ultimate resolution.

SORTING OUT DETAILS

When you have decided what the main purpose of a meeting should be, you can begin to consider the other details. Think about how long the meeting should last, and bear in mind which issues need to be discussed and the amount of time that should be allocated to each. Remember to allow time for delegation of tasks, maybe a refreshments break, and summing up. Be sure to schedule the meeting so that the right people, with the requisite levels of authority, are able to attend. If they cannot, rearrange the meeting at a more convenient time. When it comes to meetings that are held regularly, check at frequent intervals that they continue to serve a useful purpose and do not waste time.

QUESTIONS TO ASK YOURSELF

Q Is the purpose of the meeting clear to everyone?

Q Does everyone need to attend the entire meeting?

Q Is there a better way of addressing the issues than having a meeting?

Q Are there other people who do not usually attend your meetings who might make a useful contribution this time?

Q Will the meeting benefit from the use of any visual aids?

ASSESSING PERSONAL AIMS

Whether you will be chairing a meeting or simply attending one, reflect in advance on the specific objectives of the meeting as well as on your own personal aims. There may be certain items on the agenda in which you have a particular interest, for example. Clarify in your own mind what outcomes you would consider acceptable. You can then start to prepare accordingly. Another question to consider is whether you can minimize the amount of time you spend at the meeting. If you do not need to attend the entire meeting, and have decided to be present only for part of it, inform the chairperson in advance.

> **3** Consider carefully what makes a successful meeting, and what is likely to make an unsuccessful one.

REINFORCING OBJECTIVES

If you are chairing a meeting, start the proceedings by summarizing its aims and objectives, so that all the participants can keep them in mind for the duration of the meeting. Remind the participants what decisions must be reached and by when, and what information will be conveyed, and – if they stray from the point – draw their attention to the amount of time that has been allocated to the discussion of each issue. If you are simply an attendee at a meeting, ensure that you are well prepared for thorough discussion of any issues that particularly concern you.

CONFIDENTIALITY ISSUES

All parties should know at an early stage in the proceedings if they will be dealing with any confidential issues in a meeting, since this may affect the approach of the participants. All confidential items must be handled appropriately, and confidentiality must always be respected outside the meeting room. If an agenda will contain a mixture of confidential and non-confidential items, ensure that the status of each item is made clear to all of the participants in advance.

> **4** Consider what would happen if a regular meeting were not held.

▼ YOUR CRITICAL PATH
Until you have decided upon your aims, you cannot decide what sort of meeting you need. Determine them and the length of the meeting, then invite the participants.

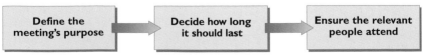

| Define the meeting's purpose | → | Decide how long it should last | → | Ensure the relevant people attend |

MEETING INFORMALLY

Informal meetings take several different forms and can be a useful forum for discussion. Whether they happen by chance or are organized in a casual manner, such as by word of mouth, make the most of these opportunities for resolving matters simply.

5 Remember that the presence of senior managers may inhibit discussion.

SETTING THE SCENE

Informal meetings, despite their casual nature, still benefit from well-chosen surroundings. A fruitful discussion is unlikely if participants feel uncomfortable, or if they are attempting to discuss confidential issues in an open-plan office. Select the right surroundings to encourage the outcome you are seeking.

6 Hold meetings away from your work space so that you can leave easily.

▼ RESOLVING ISSUES
Use an impromptu meeting, for example with a colleague in a corridor, in order to attempt to resolve an issue immediately.

IMPROMPTU MEETINGS

Meetings called at very short notice, and those that happen in passing or on the spur of the moment, are termed "impromptu". They are ideal for discussing issues frankly and reaching decisions quickly without being impeded by the presence of large numbers of people. Use them to best effect in order to resolve minor problems simply by calling together a maximum of three or four people. Alternatively, use them to make urgent announcements. Between colleagues, impromptu meetings tend to be characterized by casual verbal style and relaxed body language. Set an informal atmosphere, and this will help you to interpret the reactions of other people in the meeting. Look out for facial expressions: because participants may be off their guard, their expressions are likely to be genuine.

SMALL INFORMAL MEETINGS

Useful for discussing, problem-solving, and giving feedback, small informal meetings are planned – therefore they allow for preparation time, in contrast to impromptu meetings. Even when running a small informal meeting consisting of just two or three people, keep the purpose of the meeting and a time limit in mind. Control the meeting properly, and you can keep the subject matter moving along while at the same time allowing for open conversation between participants. Encourage this by maintaining eye contact – the most expressive form of body communication – with them.

▼ DISCUSSING ISSUES
If you are leading a discussion, make sure that you make a lot of positive eye contact to help you retain control of the meeting.

▼ SHARING IDEAS
Small brainstorming meetings are a good forum for sharing ideas freely. If you are in control of a brainstorming meeting, ask someone to note ideas down as they are mentioned. This written record often sparks off other suggestions.

BRAINSTORMING SESSIONS

Use informal brainstorming sessions to generate new ideas or elicit quick ideas for solutions to problems. For the best results, explain the purpose and time limit of the meeting in advance so that participants can prepare. Brainstorming is most effective with a small group of people who have a range of approaches and expertise, so ask everyone to contribute in turn. Avoid criticizing or judging the ideas during the meeting, since this inhibits suggestions; judge their feasibility afterwards.

MEETING FORMALLY

*E*ach *of the various different types of formal meeting has different rules of procedure. Some meetings, such as annual general meetings, must be convened by law; others are voluntary and are called to make a particular decision or to discuss an issue.*

7 Familiarize yourself with the different types of formal meeting procedure.

FORMAL MEETINGS

TYPE OF MEETING	CHARACTERISTICS
BOARD MEETING A board meeting is attended by the board of a company – usually comprising its directors. In some countries, the board must exercise its powers collectively by law.	● Board meetings usually take place at regular intervals, perhaps once a month, to discuss company business. Meetings usually take place in a board room – traditionally a formal space with a large table. ● A board meeting is chaired by the chairperson, who is elected according to the rules of the company.
STANDING COMMITTEE A standing committee is a subgroup of a company board. It may be given responsibility for recurring tasks, such as the annual review of a chief executive's salary and performance.	● A standing committee meets regularly to fulfil its delegated tasks. ● The board of a company may authorize a standing committee to act in its place. ● A standing committee may report back to a company board, which will then implement any necessary action.
ONE-OFF COMMITTEE A company board may establish a one-off committee to look at an issue that needs particular attention. Such a subgroup may meet more regularly than the full board.	● One-off committees can meet as and when necessary to discuss specific issues that require specialist expertise or to look at complicated problems in detail. ● Many company boards find it difficult to meet more than once a month; a one-off committee can meet regularly and need only involve the necessary individuals.
PUBLIC MEETING A public meeting is open to anyone. This type of forum may be used by local government or private action groups wishing to consult the public on various issues, or by companies wanting to discuss developments.	● All members of the general public are invited to attend public meetings, which are usually advertised in advance at local community centres, in public libraries, and in local newspapers or magazines. ● An agenda for a public meeting usually consists of only one main issue for discussion.

FOLLOWING THE RULES

The rules that govern formal meetings can be complicated and vary from country to country and organization to organization. Rules may dictate the amount of advance notice that must be given for a meeting, the rights of people to attend, or the procedures to be followed in the event of a vote. If you are involved in formal meetings, find out in advance what set of rules you should follow.

8 Be aware of any legal requirements that are entailed in formal meetings.

TYPE OF MEETING	CHARACTERISTICS
CONFERENCE A conference is a meeting at which several presentations are given on one theme. Some conferences are open to the public; others are for a restricted group, such as company employees.	● This type of meeting is ideal for communicating information to a large number of people at once and in a short space of time. ● Due to their size, conferences allow little scope for discussion or audience participation, although speakers may hold question-and-answer sessions.
EXTERNAL MEETING An external meeting comprises a group of people from one organization and another group from outside that organization – for example, visiting trade-union negotiators.	● Confidentiality is an important issue in external meetings. Participants should think carefully about which information must remain private and which may be disclosed in the meeting in order to achieve its ends. ● External meetings can be held on neutral ground.
ANNUAL GENERAL MEETING (AGM) An AGM is a yearly, often mandatory, gathering of a company's directors and shareholders to discuss business during the past year and future plans.	● An AGM allows shareholders to question company directors and hold them accountable for the company's performance. ● Directors use this opportunity to seek approval of annual accounts, reappoint auditors, and to discuss future plans and policies.
EXTRAORDINARY GENERAL MEETING (EGM) An EGM is a meeting that can be called at any time between AGMs if shareholder approval is needed for immediate action.	● Shareholders should be given a certain amount of notice of an EGM. How much notice varies from country to country. ● The rules governing the procedure of an EGM are usually the same as those governing the procedures of an AGM.

REVOLUTIONIZING COMMUNICATIONS

Computer and communication technology (together known as information technology, or IT) is advancing so rapidly that fewer face-to-face meetings are needed. Use these sophisticated tools to reduce the time you spend attending meetings.

9 Before a meeting, phone attendees to focus them on the issues.

VIRTUAL COMMUNICATION

Digital technology is revolutionizing traditional methods of exchanging information, greatly reducing the need for travel. Digital alternatives to face-to-face meetings include telephone conference calls; real-time, on-line video conferencing; and e-mail and Internet messages. Consider these options before scheduling distant meetings.

10 Be selective with information, and avoid overload.

VIDEO CONFERENCING

The video conference, using real-time audio and video links, is now a widely used and increasingly user-friendly way of holding a meeting. Provided you have the required technology in place, you can use these meetings, like telephone conferencing, to link individuals from all around the globe. Video conferencing has the advantage of revealing body language and facial expressions – often key elements in effective communication.

11 Take into account global time differences when organizing and setting up conference calls.

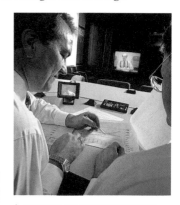

▲ VIDEO PARTICIPATION
Mix traditional and new approaches to suit you. For instance, let delegates unable to attend an actual meeting join in via video.

I2 Optimize an on-line meeting by setting a time limit.

I3 Repeat your name when you speak during a telephone conference call.

CULTURAL DIFFERENCES

Traditional barriers to cross-cultural business communication include different languages, different time zones, and travelling times between countries – as well as different cultural expectations. However, many of these difficulties are diminishing with the aid of information technology. E-mail provides a ready channel of communication, regardless of location or time zone. The widespread use of English, which can deter non-native speakers from formal communication, is less of a problem when it comes to e-mail, since messages tend to be relatively short and informal, with little need for sophisticated use of language.

E-MAIL CORRESPONDENCE

Electronic mail (e-mail) facilitates the sending and receiving of written communication via the Internet at great speed and frequency. This can amount to a different kind of meeting, extending over days and even weeks, as participants join a "virtual" conference site and comment on a current issue or problem, or discuss a range of topics. Within organizations, this enables a wide cross-section of employees from different departments – and different sites – to participate in discussions without going to the trouble and expense of meeting physically. Unnecessary information, however, can quickly accumulate. Try to keep all messages short and to the point – this will help limit the agenda of the "conference".

▼ EFFECTIVE LINK-UPS
Video conferencing allows you to communicate fully even when you cannot meet. Make the most of all tools available to you, including written material and the full range of body language.

CHOOSING THE RIGHT TYPE OF MEETING

There are many types of meeting – formal and informal – and each type suits a particular purpose. For this reason, you must decide which type is most likely to achieve your purpose before you begin to make arrangements and notify participants.

14 Always think carefully about the type of meeting you need to hold.

15 Keep meetings as small as possible to help minimize distractions.

CONSIDERING FACTORS

Once you have decided that you need to hold a meeting, the next step is to consider a number of factors, such as the urgency of the meeting. Should it be held immediately? Who needs to attend? What do you want to achieve from the meeting? Bearing in mind these questions and your core aim, choose the type of meeting that is most appropriate. For example, a one-to-one meeting or a formal committee meeting is usually best suited to decision-making, while brainstorming sessions may be good for sharing ideas.

DECIDING MEETING SIZE

The purpose of a meeting will influence its ideal size. There are advantages and disadvantages to both large and small meetings: large groups of people hold diverse opinions but the members are likely to split into cliques, whereas small groups can act together more productively but may have a narrower range of views. The popular meeting size of between six and nine participants is small enough to control, yet large enough to provoke debate. Meetings of this size encourage attendance since participants know that they will be heard.

16 Place a watch or clock in a prominent position so you are able to keep an eye on the time.

MATCHING THE PURPOSE OF A MEETING TO THE TYPE

PURPOSE	CONSIDERATIONS	MEETING TYPE
DEALING WITH INFORMATION For example, giving or receiving reports, issuing instructions, announcing and explaining procedural change.	Concerns up to three people	Informal
	Concerns four or more people or a team	Formal
	Requires feedback and discussion	Informal or formal
	Keeps company directors up to date	Formal
	Involves shareholders	AGM or EGM
	Involves informing as many people as possible outside an organization, including the media	Public
	Involves speakers providing information	Conference
RESOLVING PROBLEMS For example, handling grievances.	Concerns only one person	One-to-one
	Requires input from several people or a team	One-off committee
	Concerns urgent problem	Impromptu
MAKING DECISIONS For example, choosing between options, obtaining authorization, committing to a course of action.	Needs quick discussion, or concerns non-standard business matter	Impromptu
	Involves recurring business matters	Formal
	Requires discussion or authorization at the highest level of an organization	Board
	Requires authorization from the shareholders of a company	AGM or EGM
ENCOURAGING IDEAS For example, generating creative solutions.	Needs creative ideas to be discussed	Informal
	Needs fresh ideas to be generated quickly	Brainstorming
	Needs reports on issues to be considered, discussed, and prepared	Formal

KEEPING ON TRACK

There are various reasons why some meetings do not achieve their objectives. Attendees may have conflicting aims, the meeting may lose direction, or the agenda may be too long to cover in the time. Agreeing goals in advance will help you to reach them.

17 Circulate any supporting papers together with the agenda.

THINKING AHEAD

Before any meeting, it is important to think ahead and plan carefully to ensure that the meeting goes smoothly. First, circulate a clear agenda. Make sure that you allow enough time for the meeting so that you do not end up rushing through major items on the agenda. Identify people who may try to hijack your meeting, and anticipate their arguments. Seek out those who you think may share your opinions, and encourage them to support your case.

18 Canvass support from possible allies in advance of the meeting.

AVOIDING PITFALLS

Most of the pitfalls that arise in meetings can be avoided by good preparation and participation by all attendees. Be sure to always:

- Study all the material that has been circulated in advance of a meeting;
- Start and finish the meeting on time;
- Follow the agenda scrupulously;
- If chairing the meeting, involve others as much as possible in questions and answers;
- Make sure that participants are fully aware of the decisions that have been reached.

When the last item on the agenda – usually styled "Any Other Business" – is reached, attendees may start talking over each other, raising minor points. If you are chairing the meeting, allow everyone to have their say in an orderly fashion.

19 Make sure the aim of a meeting is agreed before the meeting starts.

20 Remind people of the agenda whenever they stray from it.

RUNNING A MEETING

POSITIVE COURSE OF ACTION		NEGATIVE COURSE OF ACTION
Prompt and positive start is made	**Open the meeting**	Participants arrive late
Discussions are kept within time limit	**Discuss issues on the agenda in turn**	Deviations from agenda occur
Attendees contribute effectively	**Obtain opinions on each issue**	Dissension between participants occurs
Acceptable solution is found		
All options are explored	**Move towards objectives**	Bickering is allowed to continue
Compromise is negotiated	**Reach a decision**	Debate ends in deadlock
Points are recapped and agreed	**Close the meeting**	Meeting is inconclusive

PREPARING FOR A MEETING

Time spent preparing for a meeting is rarely wasted.
Ensure that the right people attend, at the right
time and place, and that they reach the right decisions.

INVITING PARTICIPANTS

Choosing the right people to attend a meeting may determine whether its aims are achieved. Each participant should be attending because they can make a specific contribution, otherwise the meeting will not be making the best use of their time.

21 Consider how participants will work in a group setting.

22 Consider travel times before you schedule a meeting.

23 Rearrange a meeting if people cannot attend.

SELECTING ATTENDEES

When you are considering who to invite, certain people will probably present themselves as obvious choices. For example, if a loan is to be discussed, you should invite someone who can authorize the agreed amount. Others may be able to contribute specific skills or advice. Invite individuals whose communication skills will help the group work productively and achieve set goals. If some participants are needed only for part of a meeting, give them estimated start and finish times for the relevant items. This will save participants' time and make the meeting easier to control.

EVALUATING CONTRIBUTIONS

When you have made an initial list of participants, pinpoint the the potential contribution of each person in turn:

- Do they have information to share? For example, a sales manager reporting on customer reactions.
- Can they offer specific advice or information? For example, a production manager.
- Is their professional status is useful? For example, a lawyer in a contract dispute.
- Can they implement agreed action? For example, a finance director at a budget meeting.

24 List speakers' names by each item on an agenda.

CONSIDERING PARTICIPANTS

PROVIDING INFORMATION
An individual from one part of a company, such as production or sales, may be invited to inform other company members about progress in their department.

OFFERING ADVICE
A person's current involvement with a particular issue, or their past experience, may qualify them to offer helpful advice to other participants.

OFFERING SPECIALIZED EXPERTISE
The presence of a person with specialized skills, either from inside or outside a company, may facilitate discussion.

AUTHORIZING ACTION
Financial decisions in particular, such as signing or negotiating a new contract, may require the presence of a financial director to authorize the action.

NOTIFYING ATTENDEES

One of the hardest parts of organizing a meeting is finding an appropriate time to suit all those you wish to invite. Sometimes the easiest way to fix a meeting is to arrange for it to follow an earlier one attended by the same people. Otherwise, e-mail messages and telephone calls can go back and forth until a date is fixed. If you find that someone cannot make the proposed date, consider whether it is feasible to hold the meeting without them before you rearrange times. Always send written confirmation of the time and place.

POINTS TO REMEMBER

- Attendees should be informed clearly of the date, time, place, and purpose of a meeting.
- Attendees should understand what they will have to contribute to the meeting.
- Background papers should be sent before the meeting to all the participants.
- The venue must be suitably equipped and should be an appropriate size.

PREPARING AN AGENDA

The best way to ensure that those attending a meeting are sure about its purpose is to send them a clear agenda well in advance. There are several ways to prepare an agenda, so find and utilize the one best suited to your purposes.

25 Avoid meeting at low-energy times of day, such as straight after lunch.

COMPILING AGENDAS

An agenda for a meeting is essentially a list of items or issues that have to be raised and debated. It should be short, simple, and clear. First, gather all relevant information, then sort out which items need to be discussed and in how much detail. You may find it useful to consult with other participants. If there are many issues to discuss, assign a time limit to each to help ensure that you do not overrun the allotted duration of the meeting. How far in advance you begin to prepare an agenda will depend on how much preparation time is needed.

26 Ensure the chairperson is informed of any agenda changes.

WRITING AN AGENDA ▶
Use this simple agenda as a model when compiling agendas for similar meetings. Number each item, and assign a start time to each for the benefit of any attendees who are not needed for the entire meeting.

Each item is numbered

27 Keep an agenda as short and simple as possible.

Committee Meeting Agenda
6th July; 11 a.m.
Green Dragon Hotel

1. (11.00) Appoint a chairperson
2. (11.10) Apologies for absence
3. (11.15) Approve last meeting's minutes
4. (11.30) Matters arising from last meeting
5. (11.45) Correspondence

   (12.00) Refreshments

6. (12.15) Finances
7. (12.45) Special business
8. (13.00) Other motions
9. (13.15) Any other business
10. (13.35) Next meeting's details

Agenda is headed with date, time, and location of meeting

Start time is allocated for each item

Details of next meeting are included at end of agenda

28 Try to restrict an agenda to one sheet of paper.

POINTS TO REMEMBER

- An agenda should contain details of the meeting's date, time, place, and purpose.
- An agenda should be as specific as possible about the main purpose of the meeting.
- All participants need to know exactly what is expected of them in a meeting.
- The time devoted to each item should be indicative of its priority.
- Time allocation should err on the generous side. Nobody minds if a meeting ends early, but overrunning is unpopular.

STRUCTURING AN AGENDA

When you come to compile your meeting's agenda, try to order topics logically and group similar items together. This prevents the risk of going over the same ground again and again. Your agenda should start off with "housekeeping" matters, such as the appointment of a chairperson and apologies for any absences, before moving on to approving the minutes of the last meeting (if relevant) and hearing reports from those assigned tasks at the previous meeting. The next items covered at the meeting should be current issues – for example, the latest financial accounts and sales figures – about which the bulk of the discussion is likely to occur. Finally, allow for any other business, and plan to set the date, time, and location of the next meeting.

29 Discuss the most important items early in the proceedings, when participants are most alert.

DISTRIBUTING AN AGENDA

Once you have drafted an agenda, send it to the other participants for comments, additions, or approval. If you wish to add or delete items from a formally approved agenda, you will need to obtain the consent of the participants. They will be more likely to agree to a deletion than an addition, unless they have a particular interest in an item you wish to drop. It is not acceptable to present participants with a revised agenda as they arrive at a meeting unless last-minute events have made it necessary – for example, because of illness of the chairperson or a sudden change in financial circumstances. Distribute the final agenda as far as possible in advance of the meeting.

THINGS TO DO

1. Decide which issues need to be raised at the meeting.
2. Send a draft agenda to all attendees, inviting their suggestions for other items.
3. Incorporate any suggestions into the next draft.
4. Recirculate the agenda to all the meeting's attendees asking for their approval, and making it final.

LOCATING A MEETING

The choice of venue is vitally important to the success of a meeting. It is not only a question of comfort; participants must also feel that the place is appropriate to the occasion. This is true for all meetings, small or large, formal or informal.

30 Consider the cost in time for those having to travel long distances.

RECOGNIZING YOUR NEEDS

Try to match the location of a meeting to its aims. If one of the objectives of the meeting is to encourage two groups of people to get to know each other better, a relaxed out-of-town atmosphere may be appropriate. By the same token, do not hold a formal meeting in a messy open-plan office. For meetings within your organization, there is still a choice – you must decide whether home, neutral, or away territory is more suited to your needs.

31 Ensure that there are facilities available for any disabled attendees.

DECIDING ON A SITE

If you are arranging a meeting that requires the hire of rooms and other facilities, shop around to compare prices, especially if you are operating on a tight budget. You may find you can negotiate a discount. Locations in the centres of large cities may be convenient for most attendees, and well served by public transport, but space in a city centre will almost certainly be more expensive than a less central equivalent. An out-of-town location will provide fewer distractions for participants, which can be especially valuable if the meeting lasts for more than one day. On the other hand, the amenities of a city may help to entice people to a meeting lasting several days. Weigh up your priorities, and make your choice of location for a venue accordingly.

LEGAL CONCERNS

By law, certain people must be invited to certain meetings, such as companies' annual meetings of shareholders – although some unscrupulous companies have been known to hold meetings at inconvenient locations or times to push through unpopular proposals. It is illegal to set a date and time for an AGM that are designed to prevent the shareholders from voting, and it is illegal to stage public meetings in inaccessible places.

ASSESSING ENVIRONMENT

Physical factors play an important part in any type of meeting. Whatever the occasion, aim to make attendees comfortable enough to concentrate, but not so comfortable that they fall asleep. Check that external noise will be kept to a minimum, and heating and ventilation are effective but not excessive. Rooms in big hotels often have excellent air conditioning but little natural light, yet this can be vital for maintaining a dynamic atmosphere.

32 Make sure phone calls are diverted away from the meeting room.

CONSIDERING DIFFERENT TYPES OF VENUE

VENUE	FACTORS TO CONSIDER
YOUR OFFICE Your work station or a meeting table with a few extra chairs.	● All your reference material is at hand. ● Your authority may be enhanced. ● Telephones may ring or people interrupt.
SUBORDINATE'S OFFICE A subordinate's work space.	● May boost the status or morale of a subordinate. ● May feel physically uncomfortable for both parties if the workspace is small.
ON-SITE MEETING ROOM A company meeting room for the use of staff members.	● Avoids issues of company hierarchy that can arise when using an individual's office. ● Outsiders may interrupt to contact the attendees.
OFF-SITE MEETING ROOM A neutral meeting space outside your organization.	● Ensures neither party dominates on "home" ground. ● Can be useful if secrecy is important. ● May be expensive and be unfamiliar to everyone.
CONFERENCE CENTRE A large venue, such as a university, which is regularly available.	● Has the facilities to take large numbers. ● Can provide technical support and security if required. ● May lack opportunities for small, informal get-togethers.
OUT-OF-TOWN VENUE An office, meeting space, or hotel in another location.	● Convenient if attendees come from all over the world. ● Adds a degree of glamour to an occasion. ● Costs a lot in terms of travel, time, and accommodation.

AVOIDING PITFALLS

There are a number of reasons – some obvious, some less so – why a venue may turn out to be a bad choice. When you are inspecting and booking your venue, try to anticipate and avoid the following common pitfalls:

- More people attend than expected – there is insufficient room and people are uncomfortable;
- Fewer people attend than expected, leaving an intimidatingly large and empty space to fill;
- Air conditioning is inadequate and the room becomes stuffy, or it is on too high and not accessible for regulation;
- Technical difficulties arise because the light switches and plugs in the meeting room are not checked and labelled;
- There is a lack of service outlets, such as banks or cafés, at or near the venue.

33 Arrange potentially problematic meetings on neutral ground.

POINTS TO REMEMBER

- Unfamiliar venues should be visited at least once before a meeting.
- It is useful for a room to have windows that can be opened or closed as temperatures fluctuate.
- Speakers need to know where thermostats and light switches are located.
- Toilets and other facilities should be clearly signposted.
- Seats should be tested for comfort by sitting in them for at least 10 minutes.

34 Ask your support staff to check the availability, timetables, and seasonal variations of local public transport.

CASE STUDY

Following a company's expansion, the accounts department had problems dealing with the sales people, so the accounts manager set up a meeting, in a room convenient for the sales department, to discuss ways to work together.

However, the room was too small, and more chairs were needed. Due to lack of space, some people had to stand, blocking others' views

of the flip-chart the accounts manager was using. The air conditioning was ineffective and the windows did not open, so the room became hot and stuffy. A door was opened, but this let in noise from the office outside. The accounts manager was called away by phone. Several other people then left in annoyance. The manager returned and asked for suggestions, but few responded. No practical solutions were produced.

◀ CHOOSING THE WRONG VENUE

This case shows that, despite every good intention, a poor choice of venue actually damaged relations between two teams instead of improving them. More positive results might have been obtained had the two teams met on neutral territory, with no interruptions and enough space for all involved in the discussion.

FOCUSING ON ACOUSTICS

A well-structured meeting room does not guarantee a good meeting, but it can increase the chances markedly. Keep in mind your meeting's objectives. The main purpose of most meetings is to share information verbally with others, so good acoustics are essential. Even a handful of people in a small room can have problems hearing each other, but acoustics are especially important for meetings with numerous participants. If there is a visual element – for example, if visual aids are to be used – both acoustics and visibility must be good, and you will need to avoid placing chairs anywhere with a restricted view.

35 Find a venue that you are sure will be free from interruptions.

▶ FLOURISHING IN THE RIGHT ATMOSPHERE
A good turnout helps the atmosphere, as do good acoustics, decent lighting, and comfortable seating. If the audience is not distracted, it can attend to the speaker, who is encouraged to communicate well.

◀ PROVIDING THE PERFECT VENUE
As this case illustrates, organizing everything ahead of time plus having a test-run meant that the advertising agency could forestall any potential problems and was able to concentrate on its presentation. In addition, the agency here made a wise decision in rejecting the impressive state-of-the-art hardware in favour of older but more appropriate equipment.

CASE STUDY
An advertising agency arranged to meet a potential client to discuss a campaign. The client operated from a small, open-plan building a considerable distance away, so the agency suggested using a hotel with conference facilities that was close to the client.

A week before the meeting, a member of the agency visited the hotel to check the room and found a multimedia system and a huge table. He asked for the table to be removed and requested standard audio-visual equipment, since he knew the agency had prepared their presentation using such equipment. On the day of the meeting, the agency executives arrived early to test-run their pitch and arrange the seating in a semicircle. The blinds and air conditioning were adjusted, and refreshments ordered.

The presentation ran very smoothly, and the agency won the new account.

SEATING PARTICIPANTS

The placement of the participants in a meeting can have an enormous impact on the success of that meeting. Consider the seating arrangements in advance and, if necessary, draw up a seating plan to give a meeting the best chance of achieving its goals.

36 Consider several seating plans before choosing the most appropriate one.

MEETING ONE TO ONE

In a one-to-one meeting, the placement of the two individuals can set the tone of the meeting and influence the course of discussion. If you are holding the meeting, influence the degree of formality by arranging the seating appropriately. There are three main examples of one-to-one seating positions to choose from: supporting, collaborating, and confronting.

To find out what the other participant perceives the tone of a meeting to be, set four chairs around a table, take your seat before the other person arrives, and watch where he or she sits.

▲ **SUPPORTING**
If you wish to be supportive, sit at right angles to the other person. This helps break down barriers and allows eye contact.

◄ **COLLABORATING**
Sit next to the other person to suggest collaboration. This arrangement implies a similarity of opinions.

◄ **CONFRONTING**
Sit on opposite sides of the table to distance yourself from the other person. This position enables disagreements to be aired more freely.

37 Use a round table for meetings with an informal tone.

SEATING GROUPS

The purpose of a large meeting should determine its seating arrangements. When seating a group of people around a table, there are three basic options using two table shapes. If there is potential for negotiation or confrontation, select a rectangular table at which the two "sides" can sit opposite each other, placing a neutral chairperson in the centre of one side. To reinforce a sense of hierarchy in a meeting, seat the chairperson at the head of the table. For more informal, non-hierarchical meetings, choose a round table around which everyone can be seated as equals. If a meeting with a substantial number of people will be held in an auditorium or sizeable room, arrange the seating in rows facing the chairperson.

CULTURAL DIFFERENCES

Hierarchy is more important in some cultures than in others. In parts of Asia, age carries great weight, so the oldest person at a meeting is given the most senior position. Other cultures attach importance to titles, so that a junior vice president would never be seated in a more senior position than a president.

Chairperson sits at head of table

Least senior person is seated furthest from chairperson

Chairperson sits between team members

▲ CONFRONTING OPPOSITION
When you are discussing issues or intending to make decisions, sit parties with opposing points of view on either side of a rectangular table.

▲ INDICATING HIERARCHY
If you wish to indicate hierarchy, put the chairperson at the head of a rectangular table, and seat the other attendees in descending order of authority.

DISCUSSING FREELY ▶
Use a round table for a meeting in which open discussion takes precedence over the status of the participants.

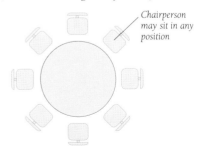
Chairperson may sit in any position

38 Make sure all the participants can see and be seen.

USING TACTICAL SEATING

The significance of seating positions depends on where the chairperson sits. Traditionally, this is at the head of the table, while the seat to the right is a privileged one. However, this need not be the case.

Tactical seating is based on an assumption that participants are influenced by the people they are near to. Decide what you want from a meeting, and arrange the seating to help you achieve this. For controversial issues, split up factions and avoid seating people with violently opposed – or very similar – ideas next to each other. This polarizes opinion and prevents the discussion from spreading. When drawing up a seating plan, base it on your knowledge and research of the attendees' views on the issues being discussed. Eye contact is crucial for indicating to members of your own team what steps you want to take next. Ask yourself who should be able to make eye contact with whom, and seat people accordingly.

39 Seat people an arm's length away from each other.

40 Avoid seating participants in direct sunlight.

▼ **DISPERSING OPPOSITION**
When drawing up a seating plan, base it on the participants' opinions on the most contentious issue being discussed. This will help to disperse opposition to the item.

Key
- 🔵 *Chairperson*
- 🔵 *Undecided*
- 🔵 *Supporter*
- 🔵 *Opponent*
- — *Sightlines*

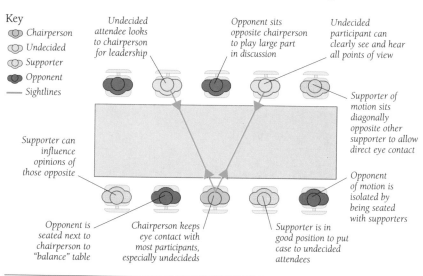

Undecided attendee looks to chairperson for leadership

Opponent sits opposite chairperson to play large part in discussion

Undecided participant can clearly see and hear all points of view

Supporter of motion sits diagonally opposite other supporter to allow direct eye contact

Supporter can influence opinions of those opposite

Opponent of motion is isolated by being seated with supporters

Opponent is seated next to chairperson to "balance" table

Chairperson keeps eye contact with most participants, especially undecideds

Supporter is in good position to put case to undecided attendees

OBSERVING SEATING

When there is no formal seating plan for a meeting, observe where other attendees sit, and select your own seat accordingly. Where someone sits may reveal how they feel about the issues under discussion and what role they wish to play in the meeting. A forceful opponent may choose a commanding position near the chairperson. Sitting in the middle may suggest a wish to participate fully or a desire to dominate the conversation at that part of the table. If you are the chairperson, try to persuade the loudest, most outspoken person to sit directly opposite you.

41 Ask attendees to turn off mobile phones and pagers.

▼ **INTERPRETING SEATING PATTERNS**
There are benefits to be gained from any seat at a meeting table, depending on what you want to achieve. Learn to "read" other attendees' aims from where they sit.

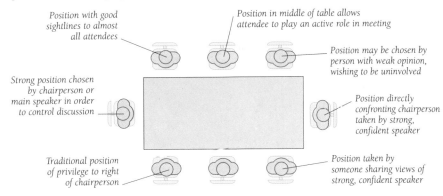

Position with good sightlines to almost all attendees

Position in middle of table allows attendee to play an active role in meeting

Position may be chosen by person with weak opinion, wishing to be uninvolved

Strong position chosen by chairperson or main speaker in order to control discussion

Position directly confronting chairperson taken by strong, confident speaker

Traditional position of privilege to right of chairperson

Position taken by someone sharing views of strong, confident speaker

42 Avoid using chairs that are too comfortable: they encourage lethargy.

PRESENTING YOUR CASE

The presentation of your case will be affected by where you sit in relation to your audience. Plan others' seating to benefit your cause. Seating an audience around you implies a collaborative and informal discussion, which may not help you sway opinions. Distancing your audience by standing in front of them, sitting on a platform, or sitting behind a desk will increase your authority and presence but may discourage two-way discussion and make it harder to gauge their mood.

PREPARING PRACTICALITIES

The success of most meetings greatly
depends on advance preparation
and organization. This includes providing
suitable facilities and materials for the
occasion – including the venue, any audio-
visual aids, and writing materials.

43 Check all audio-
visual aids are
working before
a meeting begins.

THINGS TO DO

1. Check that refreshments
have been ordered.

2. Check that the restroom
facilities are adequate.

3. Ensure that there is ample
parking available.

4. Take copies of background
papers in case some
participants have lost theirs.

5. Make sure the electrical
system is adequate.

ORGANIZING A VENUE

At your venue, you may only have a limited
amount of time available to check out the facilities,
prepare the seating, set up audio-visual aids such
as projectors and screens, and distribute agendas
or background papers. If this is the case, consider
enrolling extra help for the preparations before the
meeting and for clearing up afterwards.

When using an on-site meeting room, check the
day before the meeting that the room has not been
double-booked. Book for longer than you need for
the meeting to allow for setting up and removing
any equipment. Check that the seating facilities
are adequate for your needs, and make sure that
the room is tidy before and after the meeting.

CHOOSING AUDIO-VISUAL AIDS

Audio-visual (AV) aids are used more and more
in large meetings, presentations, and conferences
to emphasize the points under discussion.

Such aids can range from basic flip-charts
to sophisticated rear-projection video screens.
Whenever AV aids are required, always rehearse
their use before the meeting. Make sure you are
familiar with the controls, that the equipment
works, and that your aids can be seen from all
seats. If necessary, enlist technical support.

44 Beware of venues
over-catering to
make extra profit.

45 Ensure that special
dietary needs are
catered for.

Providing Writing Aids

The need for speed or accuracy when taking notes at a meeting and the style of the occasion – formal or informal – will influence participants' choice of writing aids. In certain types of meeting (press conferences, for example), attendees may use lap-top computers, personal organizers, or dictaphones to record information. In most meetings, however, notes are still taken on paper.

Provide participants with a notepad and pens or pencils to avoid the potential delays and disturbances that occur when people have to look for their own. Make this an opportunity to gain some free publicity by issuing notepads or pens imprinted with your company's logo, name, address, and telephone number.

PERSONAL ORGANIZER

DICTAPHONE

NOTEPAD AND PEN

▲ **TAKING NOTES**
Provide basic writing materials, such as notepads and pens; attendees may bring their own dictaphones or organizers.

Organizing Breaks

In the course of a long meeting, you may want to break for refreshments, even if you are providing water or hot drinks during the meeting. Use breaks to give participants a chance to discuss matters informally in small groups before reconvening. Avoid serving substantial food during breaks, otherwise attendees may become drowsy.

COFFEE

Holding Large Meetings

At a large public meeting or conference, the organization is as important as the content. Bad planning, technical hitches, and poor facilities will distract from the factual content of the meeting. Attendees are also more likely to remember your message if the event runs smoothly. Check that large numbers of people can enter and leave the venue easily, that you have set out enough seating, and that attendees can see any AV displays. Provide a public address system (PA), or separate microphones, loudspeakers, and amplifiers. Ensure that all the speakers know how to adjust and handle the equipment, and provide them with technical or any other necessary assistance.

46 Avoid consuming too much alcohol before a meeting – it rarely improves productivity.

ATTENDING A MEETING

It is the responsibility of each participant at a meeting to ensure that it attains its objectives. Prepare in advance and actively contribute to make every meeting productive.

TAKING AN ACTIVE ROLE

As a participant in a meeting, it is vital to be well-briefed. Focus on the aims of the meeting by reading the agenda and any previous minutes in advance. Consider your expected role and how you would like to contribute, then prepare accordingly.

47 Work out what you want to say before a meeting begins.

POINTS TO REMEMBER

- Background research is essential for any contribution.
- Contacting other participants before a meeting breaks the ice and allows for a useful exchange of information.
- Personal rivalries between participants must be identified.
- It may be necessary to canvass support on big issues in advance.
- Participants can be sounded out in advance of a meeting.

GATHERING INFORMATION

Carry out some basic but thorough background research before a meeting to help you to make an informed and valid contribution. Gather information by collecting new data – for instance, by talking to colleagues and experts, or reading relevant publications and research material – or by consulting old notes, minutes of meetings, or company records. Your preparation should also include some research on the other attendees. Detailed preparation at this stage will enable you to take an appropriate approach that is carefully targeted at attaining your objectives.

IDENTIFYING OPPOSITION

Before a meeting, try to discover other attendees' views on topics on the agenda, their interests, and whether any view has enough authority behind it to influence the result of the meeting regardless of the discussion. If your views are likely to meet strong resistance, try to identify your opponents and negotiate a compromise in advance, so that neither party has its authority undermined in public. It is important to understand opposing points of view to counter them successfully. You may not win over your opponents, but you should avoid deadlock.

48 Brief other participants about problem issues before a meeting.

Open body language shows willingness to listen

TALKING ▶ ISSUES OVER
It is always useful to share information before a meeting, especially for those with opposing views who may wish to talk over differences. This may help each party to tolerate and even accept other opinions.

PREPARING FOR NEGOTIATION

Negotiation is the bargaining that occurs between two parties that each possess something the other wants. The subject may not be a tangible object; it may be support for a particular course of action or assistance in performing a particular task. If you are negotiating, bring a firm goal or objective to the negotiating table – plus a strategy for achieving it. Your strategy should include points of resistance and

areas that are open to compromise. To be a successful negotiator, you must be sensitive to the needs and preferences of others. Listening to others will uncover areas of mutual agreement or weakness which you can then utilize during the negotiations. Remember that once each side has outlined their initial demands and concerns, you must both be willing to compromise in order to reach an acceptable settlement.

BEING SEEN AND HEARD

To ensure that your message is getting through to others, you should look and sound the part. Dress appropriately for each meeting, and make sure that you speak clearly and confidently whenever making a contribution to proceedings.

49 Keep your facial expression and your tone of voice positive.

LOOKING THE PART

A professional appearance can gain you extra respect when stating your case, since people tend to make instant judgments based purely on appearance. If you are attending a meeting with another company, find out about its dress code so that you are not the only participant wearing a formal suit while everyone else is in jeans. At a formal meeting, wear a formal suit, especially if you are not known to other people there. Whatever you wear, check that your outfit is clean and pressed, your hair is tidy, that your nails are clipped and neat, and your shoes are polished.

50 Videotape yourself rehearsing to check that you are being clear.

Making eye contact shows confidence

Leaning forward indicates alertness and interest

Clothes are smart and neat

Papers are kept in an orderly pile

◀ **LOOKING CONFIDENT**
This man looks confident and in control. He is well groomed and formally dressed in a well-fitting dark suit, a sober, neat tie, and a crisp, white shirt. His positive body language will leave a good impression.

GAINING CONFIDENCE

Confidence-building is a circular process. If you appear to be confident, people will perceive you as such and are more likely to be convinced by your arguments. Once you feel that other members of the meeting believe you, your confidence will increase. In any verbal communication, it is estimated that your tone of voice has five times more impact, and your body language has eight times more impact, than the actual words that you use to present your argument. Concentrate on speaking clearly and at the right time, as well as on your words and the tone of your voice. Spend at least as much of your preparation time on the quality of these presentational aspects as you do on the actual content of your speech.

51 Take a deep breath before starting to speak.

52 If an idea is your own work, take credit for it.

▼ SPEAKING FLUENTLY

Remember to put across your points clearly and succinctly. Emphasize the positive aspects of your argument rather than the negative aspects of the opposing viewpoint.

PARTICIPATING STRONGLY

The level of your participation in a meeting will depend very much on its size. If a meeting is small and intimate, you may be able to interject and make points frequently, but always make sure you have something relevant – and preferably interesting – to say. If there is a chairperson, use positive body language to show him or her you would like to speak. In a large gathering, you may get only one chance to participate. Be well-prepared so that you can concentrate on your delivery, which should be strong and succinct. In a meeting of any size, if someone tries to interrupt you or prevent you from putting forward your views, look them in the eye, use their name to get their attention, and tell them you have not finished. If they persist, seek support from the chairperson.

| Be clear | Be succinct | Be positive |

LISTENING TO OTHERS

It is just as important to listen properly in a meeting as it is to speak – sometimes even more so. Listen to each speaker's words, and consider the meaning behind them. Use clues such as body language and tone of voice to ascertain the strength of a speaker's beliefs.

53 Do not interrupt other speakers – always let them have their say.

POINTS TO REMEMBER

- Good listeners look attentive, use eye contact, do not interrupt, and show interest in what is said.
- It is off-putting to people who are trying to listen if some participants in a meeting are whispering and fidgeting.
- Irrelevant discussion should be dissuaded as soon as it starts.
- Listening involves more than just the ears. It is important also to "listen" to people's body language.

LISTENING ATTENTIVELY

When you are in a meeting, try to make the environment conducive to sharing and listening. Look interested in what the person speaking to you is saying – they may need encouragement. Do not interrupt or hurry somebody in the middle of expounding their case. It takes time to develop an argument, and it may not be fully comprehensible until the end. Avoid interrupting speakers, which can make you look foolish if your point is dealt with later. Instead, make a note of queries, and ask any questions at the end of a speech.

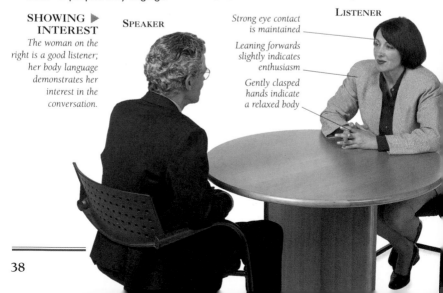

SHOWING ▶ INTEREST
The woman on the right is a good listener; her body language demonstrates her interest in the conversation.

SPEAKER

LISTENER

Strong eye contact is maintained

Leaning forwards slightly indicates enthusiasm

Gently clasped hands indicate a relaxed body

BETRAYING SIGNS OF NEGATIVE BODY LANGUAGE

As the listener, you should try to be aware of the signals you are giving out unconsciously.
If you let disbelief, impatience, or cynicism show, this may have a demoralizing effect on
a speaker who is trying to convey his or her theories and arguments to you.

SPEAKER — *Hand covers facial expression* **LISTENER**

SPEAKER **LISTENER** — *Crossed arms form a barrier*

▲ **SHOWING DISBELIEF**
*The listener's slightly open mouth implies surprise
or disbelief at what she hears. She is using her
hand to cover her mouth and hide her feelings.*

▲ **SHOWING IMPATIENCE**
*Leaning back from the speaker indicates that the
listener is distancing herself from his views. Her
tense body language reveals her impatience.*

RESPECTING OTHERS

Do not allow your personal or professional
prejudices against individual speakers to deafen
you to any good points that they may make –
always show respect for them by listening to their
comments politely, despite any reservations you
have about their ideas. This should serve you well
in the long term, as you will be accorded the same
level of respect when your turn comes to speak.

> **54** Use different
> phrases to make
> the same point
> more interesting.

TAILORING YOUR SPEECH

Listen very carefully to not only the content but
also the phrasing of everything that is said in
a meeting. You may be surprised to find that the
contributions of certain participants are closer to
what you had to say than you anticipated, or that
they may even lead you to change your plans. If
appropriate, tailor your own contribution slightly
to reflect what you have heard.

> **55** Identify any areas
> of agreement
> when you are
> negotiating.

HANDLING PROBLEMS

Problems that arise in small meetings are generally best resolved by using an open and honest approach. In a large meeting, however, problems can be more serious. A firm but fair chairperson who is familiar with procedure should be able to keep order.

56 Take personal responsibility for making every meeting a success.

57 Encourage those at routine meetings to take turns as the chairperson.

SEEING WEAKNESSES

During a meeting that has a chairperson, it is the chairperson's responsibility to maintain a neutral position and keep control. Difficulties arise if a chairperson demonstrates weaknesses, such as showing prejudice or becoming angry. Learn to see these faults so that you can take action and prevent a chairperson from losing control.

HOW A CHAIRPERSON MIGHT ABUSE THEIR POSITION

SPECIFIC ABUSES	HOW TO RECOGNIZE THEM
BIAS The chairperson defends the needs of one party in a discussion.	You may not recognize bias if it is in your favour, but if a chairperson ignores your attempts to contribute, or makes it difficult for you to do so, they may be biased against you.
INDECISION The chairperson does not lead the meeting when a decision is needed.	If a chairperson repeatedly asks for members to summarize their arguments or uses stalling tactics, he or she may not be able to reach or facilitate a decision.
MANIPULATION The chairperson does not allow the facts to speak for themselves.	Continually urging participants to reconsider a matter may be an attempt to manipulate the outcome. However, it could be a conscientious effort to get the right decision.
ANGER The chairperson does not show a calm but assertive demeanour.	Overt displays of anger from a chairperson are easily recognized, but suppressed anger may reveal itself more subtly in tone of voice or posture.

REPRIMANDING A CHAIRPERSON

If a chairperson is abusing his or her power or neglecting duties, you may need to take action – whether the meeting is formal or informal. The best way to do this is to point out what the chairperson's duties are and how those duties are not being fulfilled. State clearly what you expect the chairperson to do differently, and allow him or her the chance to remedy the situation.

58 If you reject a motion, try to find at least one area of agreement.

HOW TO REPRIMAND A CHAIRPERSON

Informal methods
- As a group, withdraw your co-operation from the meeting
- Suggest to attendees that the chairperson is behaving unreasonably
- Appeal to a superior at work to appoint a new chairperson

Formal methods
- Reconvene another meeting to appoint a new chairperson
- Inform the chairperson that they are not fulfiling their role correctly
- Suggest that the members take a vote of no confidence

SOLVING OTHER PROBLEMS

A range of other problems can impede the business of a meeting. Individual members may be badly behaved, key people may be absent, or vital information may be missing. It is the role of the chairperson to implement an acceptable solution: to restore order in the case of disruptive behaviour, to adjourn the meeting if a quorum is not formed, or to ask for more information if needed. A solution such as ejecting troublemakers can be quickly implemented by the chairperson alone; information gathering may have to involve collaborating with attendees.

59 As a chairperson, ensure that all views are heard.

TAKING MINUTES

The minutes of a meeting – short notes detailing its proceedings – are taken by the meeting's secretary as a written record of what was discussed. If you are responsible for taking minutes, ensure that they are accurate and clear.

60 Ensure that the order of minutes follows the order of the agenda.

POINTS TO REMEMBER

- Minutes should be brief, and can be written in note form.
- Prompt delivery of minutes encourages prompt action on issues raised.
- If a meeting's secretary is unclear about an issue, he or she should discuss it with the chairperson.
- Minutes should be entirely understandable to absentees.

WRITING CLEAR MINUTES

In the minutes you should record the time and place of the meeting, the names of attendees (where appropriate), all items presented, but not necessarily details of the discussions involved, and all decisions, agreements, or appointments made. During the course of a meeting, make notes from which to write the minutes in full later. Make sure the minutes are unbiased, written in a clear, concise style, and accurate. Accuracy is essential, particularly where minutes may be used as evidence in the case of a later dispute.

Date and venue are listed

Names of participants are recorded

Absentees are noted

Appointments are noted

Items presented are summarized

Minutes of 6th July meeting
Green Dragon Hotel, 11 a.m.

Present: EW, LS, RD, KS, FM, SR, DW, ST.
Absent: AR.

1. Appointment of chair: SR.
2. Minutes: approved.
3. Chairperson's review of last six months' results: things are looking good. However, the drop in revenue is disappointing.
4. Autumn sales plan: to be voted on at next meeting.
5. Report from subcommittee.

continued...

◀ **WRITING MINUTES**
When writing minutes, make sure they are brief, exact, and laid out in a legible format. Number each new point to make it obvious where one point ends and the next one begins. If the minutes are particularly lengthy, index them.

61 Suggest that your chairperson reads new minutes before they are finalized.

DISTRIBUTING AND FOLLOWING UP MINUTES

Once the minutes are complete, make sure that they are distributed quickly to all the relevant people. Compiling the minutes is a meaningless task if the action agreed on at the meeting is not duly followed up. Minutes should indicate clearly the deadlines agreed on for any projects, and who is responsible for implementation. After a suitable period but before the next meeting, follow up on the progress of any projects or tasks noted in the minutes, and update the chairperson on their status. If necessary, see that these items are included in the agenda for the next meeting.

THINGS TO DO

1. Make sure the chairperson approves the minutes.
2. Distribute minutes within a day or two of a meeting.
3. Follow up between meetings on issues requiring action.
4. Use the minutes to compile a status report on ongoing issues. Circulate it with the agenda for the next meeting.
5. At each meeting, approve the minutes of the previous meeting, and verify their accuracy with the attendees.

THE ROLE OF THE SECRETARY

Co-ordinating the minutes is the job of the secretary of a meeting. The role of secretary is an important one. The same individual can perform the role at each meeting, or the role can be handled by different people (with the exception of the chairperson, to whom the secretary is directly answerable). If you are asked to take on this role, you can delegate the administrative tasks of composing and typing the minutes as long as you supervise them carefully.

TAKING NOTES ▶
Take detailed notes during a meeting to prepare for the writing of the final minutes.

62 Write up the minutes straight after a meeting using notes taken in the meeting.

63 When writing up minutes, keep sentences short and to the point.

EVALUATING YOUR SKILL AS A PARTICIPANT

Evaluate how well you perform when you attend meetings by responding to the following statements, and mark the options closest to your experience. Be as honest as you can: if your answer is "never", mark Option 1; if it is "always", mark Option 4; and so on. Add your scores together, and refer to the Analysis to see how well you scored. Use your answers to identify the areas that most need improvement.

OPTIONS
1 Never
2 Occasionally
3 Frequently
4 Always

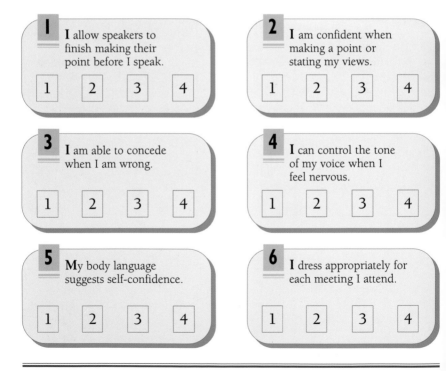

1 I allow speakers to finish making their point before I speak.

1   2   3   4

2 I am confident when making a point or stating my views.

1   2   3   4

3 I am able to concede when I am wrong.

1   2   3   4

4 I can control the tone of my voice when I feel nervous.

1   2   3   4

5 My body language suggests self-confidence.

1   2   3   4

6 I dress appropriately for each meeting I attend.

1   2   3   4

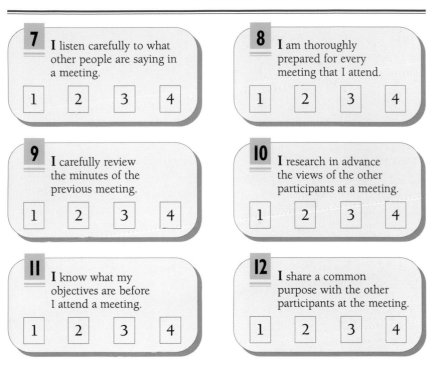

7 I listen carefully to what other people are saying in a meeting.

1   2   3   4

8 I am thoroughly prepared for every meeting that I attend.

1   2   3   4

9 I carefully review the minutes of the previous meeting.

1   2   3   4

10 I research in advance the views of the other participants at a meeting.

1   2   3   4

11 I know what my objectives are before I attend a meeting.

1   2   3   4

12 I share a common purpose with the other participants at the meeting.

1   2   3   4

ANALYSIS

Now you have completed the self-assessment, add up your total score, and check your ability by reading the corresponding evaluation. Whatever level of skill you have shown at a meeting, it is important to remember that there is always room for improvement. Identify your weakest areas, and refer to the relevant sections in this book, where you will find practical advice and tips to help you establish and hone your meeting skills.

12–24: Your skills need all-round attention. Always have a definite purpose when you attend a meeting, and endeavour to achieve it.
25–36: You perform reasonably well in meetings, but certain skills need further development.
37–48: You perform well in meetings, but do not become complacent. Continue to prepare well for each meeting you attend.

CHAIRING A MEETING

Every meeting needs a chairperson to direct the proceedings. As chairperson, you must fulfil the vital role of ensuring the smooth running and successful completion of any meeting.

UNDERSTANDING THE ROLE

A chairperson is the person in charge of running a meeting. He or she has the authority to regulate the meeting, and is responsible for enforcing any rules that govern the proceedings, keeping order, and the successful completion of business.

64 Encourage all participants to give opinions by asking open questions.

POINTS TO REMEMBER

- A chairperson is responsible for ensuring that any discussion is relevant to the points on a meeting's agenda.
- A chairperson should repeat any motion proposed by those attending to ensure that everyone has heard and understood it.
- A chairperson can expel anyone who disrupts a meeting.
- A chairperson is responsible for summing up the discussion at the end of a meeting.

USING PERSONAL SKILLS

The ideal chairperson should have a wide range of personal skills. Brush up on these essential skills before chairing any meeting:
- Firmness in running meetings to time and dealing with problems;
- Ability to summarize points succinctly;
- Flexibility when dealing with the different tones and styles of attendees;
- Openness and receptiveness when listening to opinions that you do not share;
- Fair-mindedness in ensuring that all views are aired and given equal consideration.

CHAIRING AN INFORMAL MEETING

Not all informal meetings have an "official" chairperson. Those that do usually appoint one by a vote among participants or via instructions from the meeting's organizers. The role of chairperson here is mainly to keep control and to ensure that every point of view is heard. In general, the chairperson must appear unbiased, so cannot fully join in the discussion. However, the chairperson can still exert considerable influence over the outcome of a meeting by allowing detailed coverage of some issues and limited consideration of others. The chairperson also often has a casting vote in the event of it being necessary.

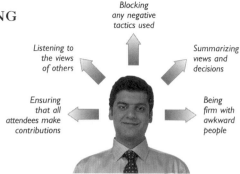

Blocking any negative tactics used

Listening to the views of others

Summarizing views and decisions

Ensuring that all attendees make contributions

Being firm with awkward people

▲ DUTIES OF A CHAIRPERSON

A chairperson can exert enormous influence on the outcome of a formal or informal meeting. It is extremely important that he or she remains neutral throughout the proceedings.

65 Ask a participant to give you honest feedback on your performance as a chairperson.

CHAIRING A FORMAL MEETING

A number of different rules govern the selection of a chairperson for a formal meeting. For example, in the case of a public company, the choice will be controlled by company rules. A government committee, however, will select its chairperson in accordance with statutory regulations. One of the main responsibilities of a chairperson is to ensure that a meeting is properly convened: that is, that the minimum number of people, known as a quorum, is present; that business follows the order of the agenda; and that there is sufficient time to discuss all the items. If these conditions are not met, any decisions taken may not be binding.

THINGS TO DO

1. Open a meeting with a short summary of its purpose and agenda.
2. Allow all parties to express their views on the subject under discussion.
3. Prevent irrelevant debate.
4. Ensure any voting procedure is followed correctly.
5. Cast the deciding vote if necessary.

RESEARCHING ATTENDEES

As chairperson of a meeting, you should familiarize yourself with the people who will be attending. Although it may not be possible to research all attendees of a large meeting, identify whether there are different factions, and be ready to deal with them.

66 Try to get to know newcomers before a meeting takes place.

RECOGNIZING INTERESTS

There is often much at stake in meetings, and discussions can become heated. Pressure groups may dominate public meetings, and there will be vocal supporters and detractors for almost every meeting about a contentious issue, such as a pay review. As chairperson, you must be prepared for any potential problems and be ready to deal with matters calmly, giving all interests a fair say, and ensuring a meeting does not get bogged down.

 67 Research any key opinion leaders thoroughly before a meeting.

UNDERSTANDING PERSONALITIES

SHY TYPE

Try to gauge if any of the attendees are likely to be nervous and lacking in confidence in a meeting. Take time to chat to them encouragingly beforehand to put them at their ease.

DOMINANT TYPE

Domineering participants with strong personalities can be very disruptive at a meeting. They should be clearly identified before a meeting so that you can control them if they start to dominate.

ACCOMMODATING PERSONALITIES

As chairperson of a meeting, you should utilize the personal skills that allow you to recognize and cope with a wide range of personalities. Spend time making enquiries about the personalities of the various participants. Shy attendees may need encouraging to participate in the meeting, while domineering attendees may have to be controlled. Remember that as chairperson you are responsible for ensuring that each participant has a fair say in the discussion.

UNDERSTANDING TACTICS

Before a strategically important meeting, key participants are likely to have planned their strategy for achieving their aims. Find out what these aims are in advance by carefully researching background information on key attendees. You will then be in a better position to anticipate and counter any negative tactics that may be employed to secure these aims. Some of the tactics used by participants may include the following: attempts to change the agenda by shifting the discussion to another subject; the undermining of less confident, opposing participants; wasting time by talking around the subject and deferring a final vote.

THINGS TO DO

1. Find out who the key participants will be.
2. Research tactics previously employed by key attendees.
3. Identify possible factions within a meeting.
4. Get to know the various personality types.
5. Familiarize yourself with the opposing views.

ANTICIPATING DISTRACTING TACTICS IN MEETINGS

TACTIC BY PARTICIPANT

DIVIDE AND RULE
This device entails the passing of conflicting information to individuals before a meeting with the intention of creating antagonisms.

DOMINATION
By speaking in a loud voice and interrupting, a dominant person may try to undermine the confidence of less dominant attendees.

BLUSTER
This time-wasting device involves somebody speaking loudly and at great length about a subject irrelevant to the one under discussion.

ANGER
Some people use anger as a tactical weapon in meetings in order to halt the discussion and have the meeting adjourned to a later date.

COUNTER BY CHAIRPERSON

RECAP ON THE FACTS
Find out who is spreading disinformation. Be prepared when in the meeting to re-establish the facts to clear up misapprehensions.

CHALLENGE THE AGGRESSOR
Research who the domineering attendees are, and be prepared to counter them in a meeting with a firm request for orderly conduct.

SILENCE THE BLUSTERER
Be prepared to isolate a potential blusterer, and counter the tactic when in a meeting by avoiding eye contact until others have spoken.

STAY CALM
Find out which attendee may use this highly disruptive tactic, and be prepared to calmly expel them from a meeting if necessary.

PACING A MEETING

Pacing a meeting correctly is an important part of the role of chairperson. Always make sure that an agenda is provided and adhered to, and that the speakers have enough time to make their points without allowing the meeting to overrun its schedule.

68 Schedule meetings before lunch – it is more likely they will end on time.

69 At the start of a meeting, inform attendees how long it is planned to last.

STARTING ON TIME

Always make a point of starting meetings on time. When you are chairing a meeting, arrive at the venue well before the planned start time. If some participants are late, start without them. However, if a key contributor is late, it is acceptable to wait for their arrival before beginning, or to change the order of the agenda to prevent delays. If starting late is unavoidable, make sure that this is noted in the minutes, along with the reasons for the delay. Do not waste time recapping for late arrivals, unless it is vital that they possess information in order to make a quick decision. Otherwise, leave it to them to find out for themselves what they have missed once the meeting has finished.

ENLIVENING THE PACE

If the pace of a meeting is flagging, take remedial action to make the most of the rest of the meeting:

● Change position and tone – stand up, and speak louder and more quickly to rouse the participants;

● Choose participants known to be lively speakers to address the meeting and generate some momentum;

● Consider skipping inessential items on the agenda – but ensure that all the participants in the meeting are in total agreement with you before taking this course of action;

● Arrange a follow-up meeting to cover any unfinished items if it becomes obvious that parts of the agenda are going to take longer than is practical.

KEEPING TO THE AGENDA

It is important to allocate an overall time limit to complete a meeting's agenda. Research shows that the attention span of most participants picks up for the first 10 to 15 minutes, then dips before rising again as the end of a meeting is anticipated. The ideal meeting length of 45 minutes minimizes loss of attention time. When chairing a meeting, keep things moving briskly by adhering strictly to the agenda, enforcing a strict time limit for each item. This establishes and maintains a sense of urgency and momentum in proceedings.

POINTS TO REMEMBER

- Attendees are usually at their most receptive at the beginning of a meeting.
- The progress of a meeting can be summarized at regular intervals.
- Reminders should be given of how much time is left to complete the agenda.
- Failure to end a meeting on time may antagonize attendees.

70 Let latecomers know their behaviour is unproductive.

USING TIME EFFECTIVELY

It is vital that the chairperson keeps a meeting's purpose clearly in each participant's mind. Do not allow participants to waste time by wandering from the point. If the discussion does begin to stray, bring it back to the main issue by saying, for example, "We are not here to discuss that today – let's get back to the point." Allow time for a brief discussion among the participants before summarizing the debate, and, if appropriate, taking a vote on the points raised in the meeting.

PROVIDING BREAKS

Time for breaks and refreshments should always be built into the agenda of a long meeting. These breaks serve several purposes: they allow attendees to discuss matters in small groups, which may help to iron out any awkward differences; they provide the chairperson with useful buffer zones that can be used to extend or shorten a meeting in special circumstances; they allow bodies and brains to relax a little. In order to achieve optimum productivity, the maximum time you should allow a meeting to run without breaks is 90 minutes.

▲ **REFRESHMENTS**
Organize the provision of refreshments during planned breaks. Avoid messy snacks, and discourage eating during the meeting.

CONTROLLING A MEETING

The key to controlling a meeting lies in anticipating problems before they arise. If you learn to interpret the body language of the participants, you can encourage the right behaviour, avoid problems, and strive for a positive and successful outcome.

71 Put a stop to any side-debates or private conversations.

READING NEGATIVE SIGNS

There are many non-verbal signs that can indicate that individuals are unhappy with the course of a meeting. Frequently checking a watch, gazing out of the window, rustling papers, and yawning all show disinterest. A closed posture – with shoulders hunched and avoidance of eye contact – discourages communication and may indicate lack of interest, but may also indicate low confidence. Watch for these signs so that you can respond appropriately, perhaps by changing the pace of the meeting.

Posture is closed

▲ **SHOWING NO INTEREST**
A lack of interest in the meeting and a low level of concentration is clearly shown in this attendee's introspective demeanour.

Fists are clenched   *Head is lowered*

◀ **REVEALING ANGER**
A displeased expression shows that this person is not happy with the way the meeting is going. His fists are clenched, he has lowered his head, and he is glaring aggressively.

Hand is pointing aggressively

72 Defuse anger by inviting participants to express the reasons for their anger.

▲ **BEING ARGUMENTATIVE**
This man has raised his hand to catch the chairperson's eye. His body language denotes a confrontational attitude.

READING POSITIVE SIGNS

There are positive signs that can unequivocally indicate that a person is happy with the progress of a meeting. An open posture with arms and hands relaxed and the body leaning forwards or towards the speaker indicates enthusiasm and encourages involvement. Sustained eye contact from an attendee shows that they are focusing their attention on you and have a positive interest in the points you are making. If you can make yourself sensitive to these signs, you will be able to use such positive body language to gauge when one or more of the participants has come to a decision. This can help you establish that the time is right to conclude a discussion or call a vote.

 73 Encourage hesitant participants with positive feedback.

 74 Watch for positive signs of interest from participants.

Raised eyebrows and slight smile are encouraging

◀ PORTRAYING INTEREST

This participant is showing interest by tilting her head towards the speaker and wearing an open expression.

Posture is alert

SHOWING ▶ ENTHUSIASM

A supportive and focused posture implies that this person is interested in what the speaker is saying.

CULTURAL DIFFERENCES

Seemingly similar expressions of body language "say" slightly different things in different cultures. In the Middle East, for example, a movement of the head upwards with a clicking of the tongue means "no". Elsewhere this represents an affirmative nod. Likewise, in India, head-shaking can mean "yes" rather than "no", while expressive hand gestures tend to be used more around the Mediterranean than in north-western Europe. Familiarize yourself with body language differences when at meetings with business people from different cultural backgrounds.

RECOGNIZING OTHER SIGNALS

As chairperson, watch for the slightest indication of unrest or lack of interest among attendees. Take action to curb disruptive signals – for example, from participants who are trying to dominate the discussion. At other times, you may have to coax introverted or reticent attendees to speak at all. Do not force shy participants to speak if you feel that they will not advance the discussion with their contribution.

Hand is raised to gain attention

◀ **WANTING TO SPEAK**
This woman is trying to contribute to the discussion. Her exaggerated gestures are an attempt to attract the chairperson's attention.

Arms are folded across body

SHYING AWAY ▶
This man does not want to be noticed. His arms are folded, and he avoids making eye contact.

ASSESSING THE MOOD

It is vital that you assess the mood of a meeting correctly when acting as chairperson. The mood can change rapidly from warm and friendly to downright hostile. If the atmosphere is tense, act quickly to improve the situation. For example, if you feel that participants are tiring of a subject, move them on to the next item on the agenda. If you feel that attendees are tiring of the meeting, conclude it by summarizing the discussion and, if necessary, calling for a final vote.

QUESTIONS TO ASK YOURSELF

Q Has everybody had a chance to express their views?

Q Have the procedural rules of the organization been followed?

Q Did you have a firm control of the meeting?

Q Did you encourage people to speak by asking them questions?

KEEPING ORDER

In a formal meeting, maintain control by ensuring that all questions and proposals are addressed through you. Anyone wishing to speak should catch your eye and request permission to "take the floor". In an informal meeting, you can also keep order by acting as a mediator for questions and debate. Do not interrupt a speaker unless they digress, overrun, or try to dominate the meeting.

75 If someone is due to speak after you, be aware if they become impatient.

WORKING TO ONE AIM

It is the responsibility of a chairperson to ensure that individual participants appreciate the interests of the whole group, personal interests are set aside where necessary, and everyone at a meeting is working towards the same aim. Make sure that this happens by firmly controlling those who stray from the purpose of a meeting, and sticking closely to the agenda.

 76 Pick out individuals, and ask them direct questions to stimulate debate.

CULTURAL DIFFERENCES

In Russian meetings, do not be surprised if the chairperson allows angry exchanges or even a walk-out by some participants. These actions are usually a ploy and do not constitute a breakdown. It is common practice for the "protesters" to re-enter a meeting and resume the discussion.

COMING TO DECISIONS

A decision can be reached either by taking a vote among participants, or by using your controlling authority and making the decision yourself as chairperson. When taking a vote in a smaller meeting, call for a show of hands or a poll. Do this several times if you want a unanimous vote. In a larger meeting, unanimity is unlikely, so agree before you start that a specific number of "yes" votes is enough to carry a motion. Gauge the mood of the meeting, and if you see a consensus in favour of a particular course of action, make the decision without a vote.

STIMULATING DEBATE

If a meeting stalls because the attendees are bored or become sidetracked from the main issue, it is the chairperson's responsibility to restart the discussion and confine it to the subject at hand. In order to do this, try directing open-ended questions to those present: for example, "Let me ask all of you, what would you have done in that situation?" Do not ask questions that require a simple yes or no. When looking for an answer, use your knowledge of the attendees to choose an articulate individual who can respond confidently to your question. Alternatively, try expressing a controversial opinion yourself to provoke further debate: for example, "I think in that situation I would have fired all the staff in the department". Make sure your comment is extravagant enough not to be taken at face value. If even this fails to reignite the discussion, do not waste time – move on to the next item on the agenda.

KEEPING ORDER

Problems of order at a meeting may arise from breaches of procedure, conflicts of interest, or even wilful disruption. As chairperson, you must ensure that the meeting is conducted in an orderly fashion and restore calm if tempers become frayed.

77 Be aware of the formal disciplinary procedures open to you in meetings.

UNDERSTANDING LIMITS

The nature of a meeting determines the limits or extent of your powers as chairperson and the types of procedure you can use to maintain order. There are two types of meeting: private and public. A private meeting is attended by select members of an organization, such as a company department. The rules of the organization determine the limits of the chairperson's power. A public meeting is open to everyone. If held in a public place, the meeting may be governed by local or statutory law and regulations. If held in a private venue, however, the meeting is bound by rules laid down by the meeting's organizers.

HANDLING A BREACH OF ORDER

A breach of order occurs when the strict procedure of a formal meeting is disrupted. Talking out of turn is a common breach. If this occurs, you should halt the debate, look straight at the talkers and invite them to share their thoughts. If this does not silence them, implement disciplinary procedures, which may culminate in their ejection.

Open hand gesture is an appeal for moderation

Eye contact is directed at principal antagonist

◀ **CALMING THE PROCEEDINGS**
If a discussion between two parties becomes overheated, stand up in order to regain control and pacify them. Your extra height will enable you to exert greater authority. Use a calm, measured tone of voice.

DEFUSING ARGUMENTS

When a debate becomes heated, thoughtless or personal comments may be used as ammunition, leading to increased friction and argument. Defuse arguments by guiding the discussion back to the issues and away from the personalities involved. Mediate to clear up any misunderstandings: "I'm sure Jean did not mean to say…", for example.

78 Enforce a moment's silence to bring a meeting to order following a dispute.

HANDLING SPECIFIC PROBLEMS IN A MEETING

PROBLEMS	POSSIBLE RESPONSES
EXCUSES Participant makes excuses such as, "I forgot", or "That was not my responsibility", when presenting an uncompleted task.	● Remind the participant in front of their peers that they will be expected to perform the task in future. ● Appoint someone to supervise the participant and ensure that they complete the work. ● Transfer the responsibility to someone else.
AMBUSH Participant makes an attempt to undermine the proceedings, so that the meeting does not achieve its specified purpose.	● Isolate the ambusher by drawing attention to their tactics. ● Adjourn the meeting if the participant continually attempts to interrupt discussion. ● In extreme circumstances, eject the ambusher from the meeting.
CONFRONTATION Participant adopts an unnecessarily negative and hostile attitude to opinions expressed in the meeting, and provokes argument.	● Remind the antagonist of the purpose of the meeting and the need to reach agreement. ● Stick to the facts, and encourage participants to discuss these in a calm manner. ● Introduce humour to defuse the situation, but not at the expense of the antagonist.
SERIOUS DISORDER  Participant becomes abusive, unruly, or even physically violent, or causes the meeting to descend into chaos.	● Call for order. ● Ask the participant to leave, or have him or her removed. ● Adjourn the meeting without setting a date to reconvene.

79 Ensure you are aware of the rules of each meeting.

POINTS TO REMEMBER

- The rules and regulations that govern a meeting will vary according to the meeting's location and its participants.

- Certain behaviour at a meeting, such as slander, may contravene criminal law as well as the meeting's own rules.

- Legal procedures can be used to block, as well as facilitate, the business of a meeting.

- Regulations are effective only when they are enforced properly and followed consistently.

PREVENTING DISRUPTION

When a meeting is disrupted, you must deal with the problem swiftly so that business can continue. The nature of the meeting will determine the most appropriate method of restoring control.

It is easy to control a small informal meeting while maintaining a low profile. If a meeting descends into chaos, you can invoke disciplinary procedures, adjourn until order is restored, or eject the troublemakers in the case of serious disorder. It is difficult to restore order in a large meeting, especially when a disruption has been planned in advance. Take firm control from the outset to establish your authority and discourage trouble.

80 Try to isolate troublemakers in a meeting by getting the majority of participants on your side.

USING LEGAL PROCEDURES

Legal procedures can be used to control or direct the business of any meeting. These procedures reflect the legal powers invested in a chairperson by the rules of a meeting. You must be aware of the legal procedures at your disposal in order to chair a meeting effectively. Your legal control over voting is a very important power, so check your rights with your company lawyers in advance of the meeting. If an acrimonious debate seems to be spinning out of control, you may be able to insist that the matter is resolved by a vote. As chair, you may also have a second or casting vote in cases of deadlock. Legal procedures can be used to govern the behaviour of participants at a meeting; rulings may limit certain language or actions. If necessary, institute procedures to bring a meeting to a close.

CULTURAL DIFFERENCES

In Japan the chairperson's role is to achieve a consensus of opinion. This often involves the chairperson withdrawing from the proceedings to allow participants to work their way slowly towards a solution. In the US, however, the chairperson is expected to drive the meeting to an agreement using charisma and force of personality. Power is more obviously wielded to keep order and achieve objectives.

MANAGING A TROUBLEMAKER IN A MEETING

POSITIVE OUTCOME   NEGATIVE OUTCOME

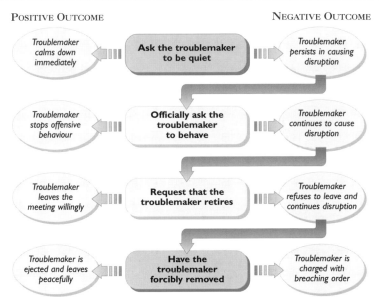

Troublemaker calms down immediately	Ask the troublemaker to be quiet	Troublemaker persists in causing disruption
Troublemaker stops offensive behaviour	Officially ask the troublemaker to behave	Troublemaker continues to cause disruption
Troublemaker leaves the meeting willingly	Request that the troublemaker retires	Troublemaker refuses to leave and continues disruption
Troublemaker is ejected and leaves peacefully	Have the troublemaker forcibly removed	Troublemaker is charged with breaching order

81 To change the atmosphere of a meeting, change the subject.

82 Eject any troublemakers only as a last resort.

ADJOURNING A MEETING

If the disorderly conduct of participants leads to their expulsion and a quorum (the minimum number of attendees required for a formal meeting) is no longer present, a meeting may be adjourned. There are specific rules of procedure that can be invoked to adjourn a meeting in the case of a dispute or outbreak of disorder. However, you can use your discretion when deciding on the length of an adjournment. A meeting can be adjourned for a short period, such as half an hour, to allow tempers to cool. Alternatively, if a disruption is more serious, a meeting can be postponed indefinitely – an adjournment *sine die*, (literally, without a day). In this case, no future time or place is fixed to continue the meeting.

CLOSING A MEETING

When all the items on an agenda have been discussed, and any necessary action agreed, it is the duty of the chairperson to bring the proceedings to a close. Ensure that all decisions are recorded accurately and any follow-up procedures are set in motion.

83 Arrange the next meeting while all the participants are present.

THINGS TO DO

1. Conclude Any Other Business.

2. Summarize discussions and recap decisions.

3. Inform participants of the time and venue of the next meeting if it has been booked and confirmed.

4. Ensure that any outstanding items are noted for inclusion at the next meeting.

DEALING WITH ANY OTHER BUSINESS

The final item on the agenda of most meetings is Any Other Business (AOB). This gives participants an opportunity to raise issues that could not have been anticipated before the meeting, such as points stimulated by the discussion.

Participants sometimes use AOB tactically to raise controversial issues or to introduce surprise or unexpected items to a meeting. As chairperson, you must decide whether to allow this practice. You may either permit a discussion or vote on the issues raised under AOB, or add the issues to the agenda for the next meeting so that they can be discussed fully before a decision is made.

CASE STUDY

Jim heard that his company's main rivals, Digby, were shifting their freight from road to rail. At a company meeting, he suggested doing the same.

Aziz, a partner, said that rail made sense for Digby, which had a lot of business abroad, but for their own domestic business, road transport was better. Another partner, Frank, said he thought Digby had shifted all its freight to rail and agreed a special deal as a result.

Their fourth partner, Sally, suggested looking at the benefits of a full versus a partial shift to rail. Her motion was seconded and passed. When summing up the chairperson raised and recapped the subject.

After the meeting, the task of researching the subject was passed to David, a junior colleague. Although he had not attended the meeting, he studied the notes on the motion and then was able to prepare a preliminary report.

◀ **PROPOSING MOTIONS**
Although Jim's proposal was not accepted unequivocally, it led to constructive action. Because it had been recorded in detail as the meeting was being closed, a colleague who had not even been present at the discussion was able to take the matter up and research it thoroughly.

SUMMARIZING DECISIONS

Once participants in a meeting have considered the final item of business, recap on each decision reached, summarizing the discussion leading up to it. This is an opportunity for you to redress the balance of the meeting by giving each of the issues discussed the significance you think they merit. For example, if the most insignificant item on the agenda has inspired the longest, most heated debate, give it scant attention in your summary to indicate the weight you think it deserves. Summing up will also highlight any issues that require further discussion at a future meeting.

84 Ensure decisions are all recorded in writing.

85 Always try to end a meeting on a positive note.

86 Thank everybody for attending and all the speakers for contributing.

CONCLUDING A MEETING

After summarizing the business of a meeting, decide whether you need to meet again, and set a date and time if necessary. You can confirm these details and the venue when you circulate a new agenda. The meeting can now be closed. At this point, you should thank all the participants for attending, especially if they have voluntarily given up their time to do so. This is common courtesy, but is also designed to encourage attendance and positive participation at future meetings.

FOLLOWING UP AFTER A MEETING

Your role as chairperson does not cease at the end of a meeting. Your ongoing responsibilities include:
● Approving the minutes;
● Ensuring that the secretary follows up and monitors any action agreed to be undertaken at the meeting;
● Receiving progress reports from the secretary on decisions made at the

meeting, and informing the other participants of advances if necessary;
● Encouraging participants to submit in advance any business they wish to be discussed at the next meeting;
● Setting the agenda for the next meeting, including any items that arose during discussion at the previous meeting, or that were missed or not covered fully.

USING FORMAL PROCEDURE

ormal procedure provides a ready-made framework for running a meeting. The use of set procedures can help a meeting achieve its objectives by setting out certain etiquette. Learn to use them properly, and they will help you control any meeting.

87 Distinguish between written rules and unwritten rituals.

ORDER OF PROCEDURE

Open meeting

↓

Approve previous minutes

↓

Deal with routine business

↓

Propose motions

↓

Deal with motions

↓

Pass resolutions

↓

Close meeting

OPENING FORMALLY

Before opening a formal meeting, ensure that the following conditions have been met:
- Full and proper notice has been given to all necessary attendees;
- A quorum (the minimum number of people required) is present;
- Both you and the quorum are at the venue within a certain time of the scheduled start.

If any of these stipulations are not met, you may adjourn the meeting to another time and place, or delay it for a short time if you have received notification that the missing participants are soon to arrive. If all the criteria have been met, begin the meeting by calling everyone to attention, making any necessary formal introductions, and commencing with the agenda.

**SIGNING ▶
A REGISTER**
A register of attendees is kept at company AGMs and other formal meetings. Arrivals must sign the register to record their attendance before entering the meeting.

APPROVING MINUTES

Gaining approval for the minutes of the last meeting is one of the first tasks of any regular formal meeting. In general, this process is passed over quickly. As the chairperson, you must ensure that everyone agrees that the decisions have been recorded accurately. Do this by asking for a show of hands from the floor. The value of the minutes as the official record of a meeting is worthless if somebody subsequently claims that events were different from the way they were recorded.

88 Make a tape recording of a formal meeting to help ensure that the minutes are accurate.

DEALING WITH ROUTINE BUSINESS MATTERS

As chairperson of regular meetings, part of your responsibility is to deal with routine business matters – for example, overseeing the appointment of external auditors in an AGM, reviewing your company's financial statements, or considering reports from standing subcommittees with specific areas of responsibility. Raise each routine matter on the agenda, and elicit the approval of the attendees as swiftly as possible before moving on to the next point. Record each decision for inclusion in the minutes, then move on to non-routine matters, which should take up the majority of the meeting.

89 Provide a message-taking service for participants.

90 Deal with routine and administrative matters first.

PROPOSING MOTIONS

In formal meetings, deal with non-routine business on the agenda through motions – statements of a desire to do something. (In company meetings, the terminology may be different.) Ensure that all motions are made in writing, well in advance of the meeting. Check that they have been proposed and seconded before the meeting begins, so that you do not waste time discussing an issue that has no support among the participants, and that they appear on the agenda, phrased concisely.

91 Set up an information desk next to the registration area.

92 Stand to exercise your authority at rowdy meetings.

AMENDING A MOTION

Any motion may be amended. Put forward an amendment as you would a motion, discuss and approve it, and then move on to discuss the amended motion. Although advance notice of amendments is required procedurally in formal meetings, they can be made during the course of debate in less formal meetings.

DEALING WITH MOTIONS

Always deal with motions in the order that they appear on the agenda; introduce each motion, and open the discussion to the meeting. In your role as chairperson, it is important for you to keep a tight control on proceedings, direct any debate, and encourage all attendees to participate. If necessary, consider adjourning the meeting to seek further information from expert sources.

As chairperson, you have the power in certain situations to introduce emergency motions on important issues if there has been no time to put forward a motion in advance. It is not, however, possible for you to withdraw a motion from the agenda of a meeting without first obtaining the unanimous consent of all the participants.

Once a motion has been fully debated, you will be required to put it to vote in order to reach an agreement on any action to be taken. It is vital to understand the various voting majorities demanded in different situations for a motion to be passed.

PASSING RESOLUTIONS

Voting on a motion leads to the passing of a resolution – a written indication of action to be taken in the future. As chairperson, take a vote by asking for a show of hands on each motion as you go through the agenda. If there is no dissension, pass the motion, and record it as a resolution. This can then be rescinded only if a counter-motion is put forward at a subsequent meeting. You have the casting vote in case of a tied result following debate of a motion. When a motion calls for a secret vote, ask for written votes to be placed in a ballot box, and count them at the end of the meeting, announcing the result at a later date. If agreement cannot be reached, amend the original motion and arrange to discuss it in the future.

93 Draw up clear guidelines for subcommittees.

94 Avoid using too many formalities – they may inhibit free discussion.

APPOINTING SUBCOMMITTEES

The chairperson is instrumental in appointing any subcommittees needed to take responsibility for issues that require particular consideration. For example, as chairperson of a company board, you may choose to set up a subcommittee to discuss the remuneration package of the directors. Such groups can be a subset of the main committee or experts in a specific field who are drafted in from outside, such as management consultants or industry leaders. In both cases, their function is to assist an existing committee in reaching an informed decision quickly and efficiently.

BRIEFING A ▶
SUBCOMMITTEE
It is important that a subcommittee knows what is required of them. When briefing subcommittee members, provide a clear written report, and explain it carefully to them.

CLOSING FORMALLY

Before you can close a meeting formally, a motion that it be ended must be proposed. When this has been seconded and voted on, request a vote by a show of hands from those in favour of the motion. You may choose to ask for a show of hands from those against the motion, which will help you to identify any participants wishing to extend the meeting for further discussion (for example, because they disagree with a particular decision reached during the meeting). As the chairperson, you need not allow everyone who wants to speak to do so, nor should you permit participants to speak for too long. It is at your discretion how long you permit discussions to continue before you formally close the meeting.

95 Refer complex issues to a working party that reports back at a later date.

96 Remember, you have the power to decide when a meeting closes.

SOLVING PROBLEMS IN FORMAL MEETINGS

The problems that arise in large formal meetings can be very different from those that occur at small informal events. As chairperson, you will need to resolve problems and ensure that procedure is followed so that meetings can progress smoothly.

97 Record important meetings on video to use for future reference.

HANDLING PROBLEMS USING FORMAL PROCEDURES

PROBLEMS	CORRECT PROCEDURE
LACK OF A QUORUM The minimum number of participants needed to validate a decision is not present.	Adjourn the meeting, specifying the date on which it must reconvene. Quorum requirements are variable so they need to be checked.
DISRUPTIVE PARTICIPANTS The attendees behave in a disorderly or disruptive manner and invite expulsion.	Obtain the consent of the other members of the meeting before trying to eject the disruptive participants.
WALK-OUT As chairperson, you decide to walk out of a meeting before the agenda is concluded.	The meeting must appoint a new chairperson as quickly as possible, otherwise it will automatically be terminated.
MERGER OR ACQUISITION PROPOSAL A company's share capital may become unstable when it faces a hostile bid or buy-out.	To approve the bid, you must pass special resolutions, which require the approval of a specific percentage of the shareholders.
TAKEOVER BID BY SHAREHOLDERS Shareholders attempt to take over a company by accumulating the majority of the shares.	Check the company's rules to establish correct procedure. If the company is quoted on a stock exchange, the exchange's rules apply.
WINDING UP A COMPANY A company can be wound up for failing to pay its debts or not fulfilling its original purpose.	Inform the shareholders that they must apply to the courts in order to wind up the company with the correct legal process.

98 Simplify procedural rules wherever possible.

99 Keep calm during demonstrations, and they may defuse themselves.

USING SET PROCEDURES

Always fall back on procedure when a problem arises. Referring to procedure helps you uphold the rights of the participants and manage the meeting effectively. Remember that:

- There are always rules to control an unruly meeting, implement action, or force a resolution;
- Most formal procedures have a basis in law, or have been established by a governing body or a meeting of members;
- Most formal procedures are to ensure that all of a company's shareholders are treated equally;
- All participants should have access to the rules governing procedure so that they are aware of their obligations and rights.

ADAPTING PROCEDURES

You are responsible, as chairperson, for ensuring that participants do not exploit procedures for their own advantage. It may be worth simplifying complicated procedures and tightening loopholes to deter abuse. The process for changing rules or procedures depends on the company: you, as chairperson, may be able to do it yourself, or it may require a vote. Some companies in the US have attempted to protect themselves from takeovers by adopting procedures that make acquisition bids prohibitively expensive. A temporary change in rules can ensure smooth running of a meeting, but permanent procedural changes should be made with care. Remember that your role as chairperson is to protect the long-term interests of members.

101 Discuss in advance with security staff what the procedure is for dealing with troublemakers.

 100 Call a short adjournment if tempers flare.

POINTS TO REMEMBER

- The chairperson is ultimately responsible for the smooth running of a meeting.
- The chairperson should never become involved in argument.
- Security staff should be on-hand at all times, but without being too intimidating or over-zealous.
- If the tempers of participants erupt, they should be calmed immediately. If they refuse to settle down, they should be removed from the venue.
- Exits should be left clear for ejecting troublemakers.

EVALUATING YOUR SKILL AS A CHAIRPERSON

Evaluate how well you perform as a chairperson by responding to the following statements, and mark the options that are closest to your experience. Be as honest as you can: if your answer is "never", mark Option 1; if it is "always", mark Option 4; and so on. Add your scores together, and refer to the Analysis to see how you scored. Use your answers to identify the areas that need most improvement.

OPTIONS
1 Never
2 Occasionally
3 Frequently
4 Always

1 I begin each meeting at its scheduled start time.

1   2   3   4

2 I ensure that participants understand the minutes of the previous meeting.

1   2   3   4

3 I follow the approved agenda for each meeting.

1   2   3   4

4 I explain the purpose of each meeting clearly to all the participants.

1   2   3   4

5 I allow all points of view to have a fair hearing.

1   2   3   4

6 I am aware of each participant's motives and hidden agendas.

1   2   3   4

7 I ensure that all participants are fully involved in each meeting.

| 1 | 2 | 3 | 4 |

8 I make sure that I am thoroughly prepared for each meeting.

| 1 | 2 | 3 | 4 |

9 I refer to a meeting procedures guide before each formal meeting.

| 1 | 2 | 3 | 4 |

10 I make sure that full and accurate minutes of each meeting are taken.

| 1 | 2 | 3 | 4 |

11 I ensure that participants know what action to take before the next meeting.

| 1 | 2 | 3 | 4 |

12 I ensure that participants know the time and place of the next meeting.

| 1 | 2 | 3 | 4 |

ANALYSIS

Now you have completed the self-assessment, add up your total score and check your performance by reading the corresponding evaluation. Whatever level of success you have achieved chairing meetings, it is important to remember that there is always room for improvement. Identify your weakest areas, and refer to the sections in this book where you will find practical advice and tips to help you to hone your skills as a chairperson.

12–24: Your skills as chairperson need considerable improvement; rethink your approach to the role, and take action.

25–36: You have definite strengths but must concentrate on improving weak points.

37–48: The meetings you chair should run smoothly. But each meeting is different, so continue to prepare well.

INDEX

ACKNOWLEDGMENTS

AUTHOR'S ACKNOWLEDGMENTS

The production of this book has called on the skills of many people. I would like particularly to mention my editors at Dorling Kindersley, and my assistant Jane Williams.

PUBLISHER'S ACKNOWLEDGMENTS

Dorling Kindersley would like to thank Emma Lawson for her valuable part in the planning and development of this series, everyone who generously lent props for the photoshoots, and the following for their help and participation:

Editorial Tracey Beresford, Marian Broderick, Anna Cheifetz, Michael Downey, Jane Garton, Adèle Hayward, Catherine Rubinstein; **Design** Helen Benfield, Darren Hill, Ian Midson, Simon J. M. Oon, Kate Poole, Nicola Webb, Ellen Woodward; **DTP assistance** Rachel Symons; **Consultants** Josephine Bryan, Jane Lyle; **Indexer** Hilary Bird; **Proofreader** David Perry; **Photography** Steve Gorton; **Additional photography** Andy Crawford, Tim Ridley; **Photographers' assistants** Sarah Ashun, Nick Goodall, Lee Walsh; **Illustrators** Joanna Cameron, Yahya El-Droubie, Richard Tibbetts.

Models Felicity Crowe, Patrick Dobbs, Carole Evans, Vosjava Fahkro, John Gillard, Ben Glickman, Zahid Malik, Sotiris Melioumis, Mutsumi Niwa, Mary-Jane Robinson, Kiran Shah, Lois Sharland, Daniel Stevens, Fiona Terry, Gilbert Wu; **Make-up** Elizabeth Burrage.

Special thanks to the following for their help throughout the series:
Ron and Chris at Clark Davis & Co. Ltd for stationery and furniture supplies; Pam Bennett and the staff at Jones Bootmakers, Covent Garden, for the loan of footwear; Alan Pfaff and the staff at Moss Bros, Covent Garden, for the loan of the men's suits; David Bailey for his help and time; Graham Preston and the staff at Staverton for their time and space; and Anna Youle for all her support and assistance.

Suppliers Austin Reed, Church & Co., Compaq, David Clulow Opticians, Elonex, Escada, Filofax, Mucci Bags.

Picture researcher Mariana Sonnenberg; **Picture library assistant** Sam Ward.

PICTURE CREDITS

Key: *b* bottom, *c* centre, *l* left, *r* right, *t* top
Powerstock Photo Library 15*br*, 27*cr*. **Tony Stone Images** jacket front cover *tr*, 4–5, 14*br*.

AUTHOR'S BIOGRAPHY

Tim Hindle is founder of the London-based business language consultancy, Working Words, which helps international companies to compose material in English and communicate their messages clearly to their intended audiences. A regular business writer, Tim Hindle has been a contributor to *The Economist* since 1979 and was editor of *EuroBusiness* from 1994 to 1996. As editorial consultant and author, he has produced a number of titles including *Pocket Manager, Pocket MBA,* and *Pocket Finance,* and a biography of Asil Nadir, *The Sultan of Berkeley Square.*